METALS
AND THE ENVIRONMENT

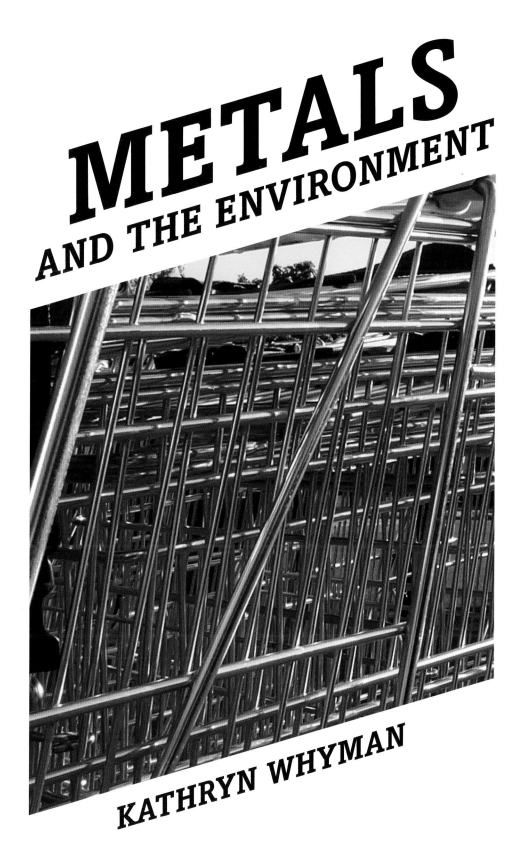

KATHRYN WHYMAN

Franklin Watts
London • Sydney

© Archon Press Ltd 2003

Produced by
Archon Press Ltd
28 Percy Street
London W1T 2BZ

New edition first published in
Great Britain in 2003 by
Franklin Watts
96 Leonard Street
London EC2A 4XD

Original edition published as
Resources Today – Metals and Alloys

ISBN 0-7496-4758-2

A CIP catalogue for this book is
available from the British Library

Printed in U.A.E.
All rights reserved

Editor:
Katie Harker

Designer:
Phil Kay

Illustrators:
Louise Nevett
Simon Bishop

Picture Researcher:
Brian Hunter Smart

CONTENTS

Metals around us	4
Where are metals found?	6
Mining for metal	8
Iron	10
Making steel	12
Aluminium	14
Copper and its alloys	16
Mercury – liquid metal	18
Precious metals	20
Shaping metals	22
Cutting and joining	24
The environment	26
Modern metals	28
Metal deposits	30
Glossary	31
Index	32

METALS AROUND US

Metals play a very important part in our modern world. We use metals for building houses, bridges, making drink cans and jewellery. Some are used in huge amounts, like iron and aluminium. Others are used in small amounts, like tungsten and palladium.

Nuclear power stations and nuclear weapons also use metals, such as uranium and plutonium. These metals create huge amounts of radioactive energy.

Copper cables are used to transport electricity across long distances – these cables are supported by large steel pylons

What is a metal?

The world is made up of thousands of different substances – water, salt and wood are just a few examples. These substances are made up from one or more of about 100 basic substances – called 'elements'. Seventy elements are metals. Metals are usually shiny, strong and good conductors of heat and electricity.

Environmental concerns

Our use of metals can be costly to the environment, unless properly controlled. Open cast mines can scar the landscape and destroy natural habitats; processing metals can release huge amounts of chemicals into the atmosphere; discarded metal is an eyesore; and at present the disposal of radioactive metals is unsatisfactory.

WHERE ARE METALS FOUND?

Metals are found as minerals (or 'ores') in the ground. A few metals, such as copper, gold, silver and platinum, are found as pure metals. But most metals are found combined or joined with other substances scattered thinly in the rocks of the Earth.

Metals can be found in most places but only ores rich enough in metals are worth mining. Geologists can test areas where these ores can be found. Getting metals out of the rocks uses enormous amounts of energy. The supply is limited, so it is vital to conserve metals for the future.

This rock has been drilled from the ground to test for gold

Forming metals

In the rocks there are pools of molten rock called magma. As the magma cools, rocks begin to form. Any liquid left is a mixture of very hot water and minerals. This mixture may (1) react with nearby rocks and deposit minerals. The hot water may (2) seep into cracks in the rock layers, (3) react with rocks such as limestone or (4) seep through volcanic lava.

Rainwater (5) may seep into the rocks, pick up minerals and deposit them in cracks. Ancient sea water trapped in rock layers may warm up and deposit minerals in cracks (6) or seep through the sea bed as springs (7). Flowing water (8) may carry minerals and deposit them on the sea bed.
The inset shows how a typical deposit of minerals may look with the surrounding rocks removed.

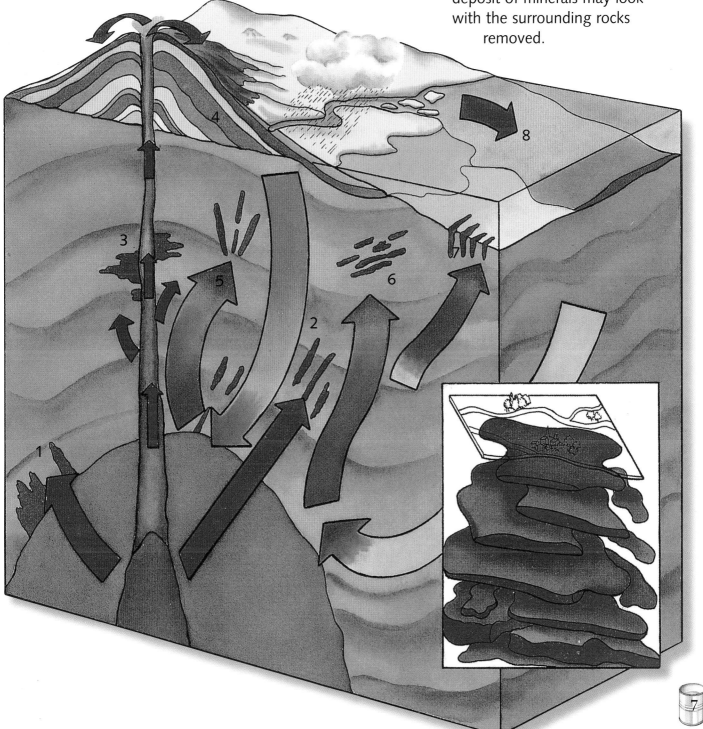

MINING FOR METAL

Metals are extracted (or 'mined') from the Earth in different ways. 'Open-cast mining' is used where soft ores, such as copper, iron and aluminium, are found near the surface. The ore is loosened and broken up with explosives before it is loaded on to trucks.

Other ores are dug from tunnels hundreds of metres below the surface. This is called 'underground mining' and is more difficult than mining at the surface. Miners dig a deep shaft into the Earth and blast the ore free with drills or explosives before taking the ore to the surface. Dredging is another method used to collect metals that are deposited in rocks in river beds or other sources of water.

Some gold mines in South Africa are over 3,800 metres deep

Dredging for tin in Malaysia

Open-cast copper mining – the copper ore is excavated and carried to waiting wagons

IRON

Of all the metals, iron is the most important to us. This is mainly because it can be made into the alloy 'steel'. Iron is one of the most widely available metals – more iron is produced each year than all the other metals put together.

Iron ore is often found combined with other substances, such as oxygen, silicon, sulphur or carbon. The metal is usually separated from these substances in a blast furnace. The intense heat of the furnace makes a fairly pure molten iron.

Most of the molten iron is used for making steel; some is further used as cast iron or as wrought iron.

Iron can also be smelted in an electric furnace

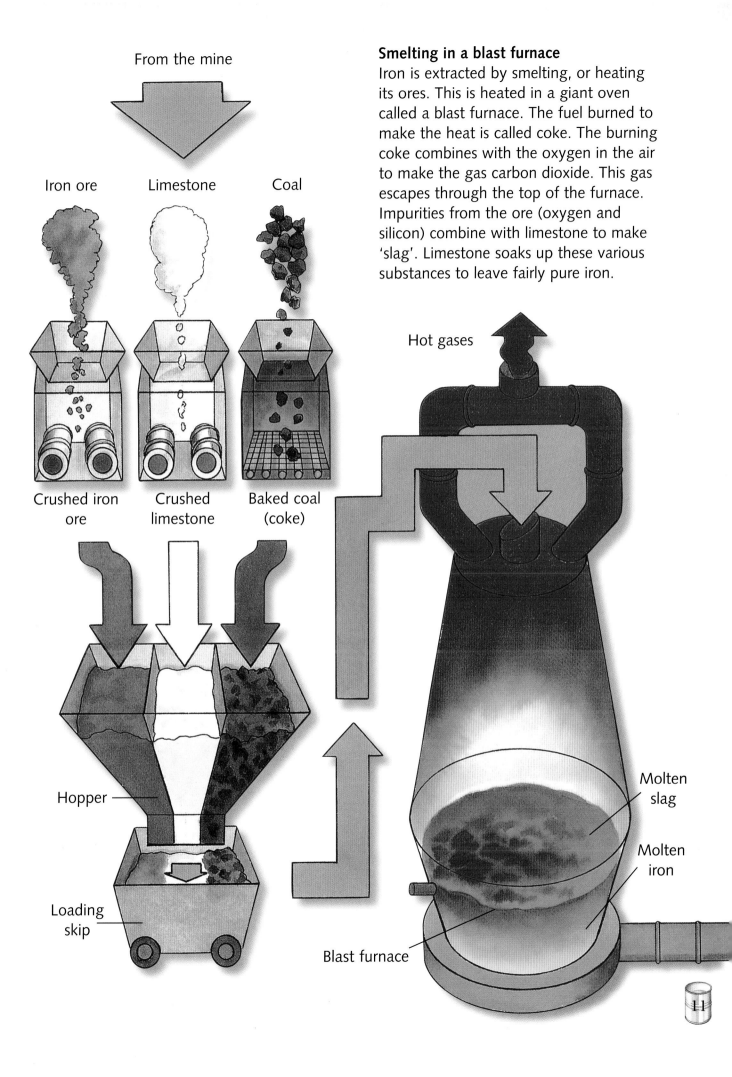

From the mine

Iron ore

Limestone

Coal

Crushed iron ore

Crushed limestone

Baked coal (coke)

Hopper

Loading skip

Smelting in a blast furnace

Iron is extracted by smelting, or heating its ores. This is heated in a giant oven called a blast furnace. The fuel burned to make the heat is called coke. The burning coke combines with the oxygen in the air to make the gas carbon dioxide. This gas escapes through the top of the furnace. Impurities from the ore (oxygen and silicon) combine with limestone to make 'slag'. Limestone soaks up these various substances to leave fairly pure iron.

Hot gases

Molten slag

Molten iron

Blast furnace

13

MAKING STEEL

Iron is a brittle metal and can easily crack. This is because it contains carbon. But iron can be used to make steel. Steel is a mixture of substances (an 'alloy'). It contains less carbon than iron and is therefore a stronger, more flexible metal.

There are many types of steel alloy, made from combining different metals and substances. Steel alloys are widely used in buildings, cars, kitchen utensils and other mass produced products. Steel is also recyclable. During the steel making process, scrap iron and molten iron is added in varying quantities.

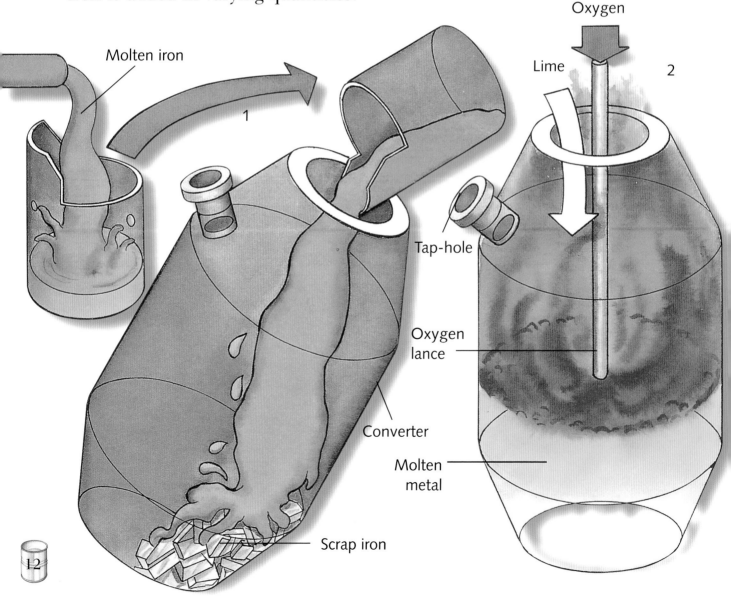

Molten iron

1

Oxygen

Lime

2

Tap-hole

Oxygen lance

Converter

Molten metal

Scrap iron

Steel production

• Molten iron is poured into a huge conical vessel called a 'converter' where it is mixed with scrap iron (1).

• A jet of pure oxygen is then blasted on to the liquid metal at great speed (2).

• The oxygen gets into the metal and burns the carbon until the right amount is left.

• Lime combines with impurities in the iron to make slag. This floats on top of the newly made steel.

• The converter is tipped and the steel and slag are poured into separate ladles (3&4).

A jet of pure oxygen burns carbon from molten iron to make steel

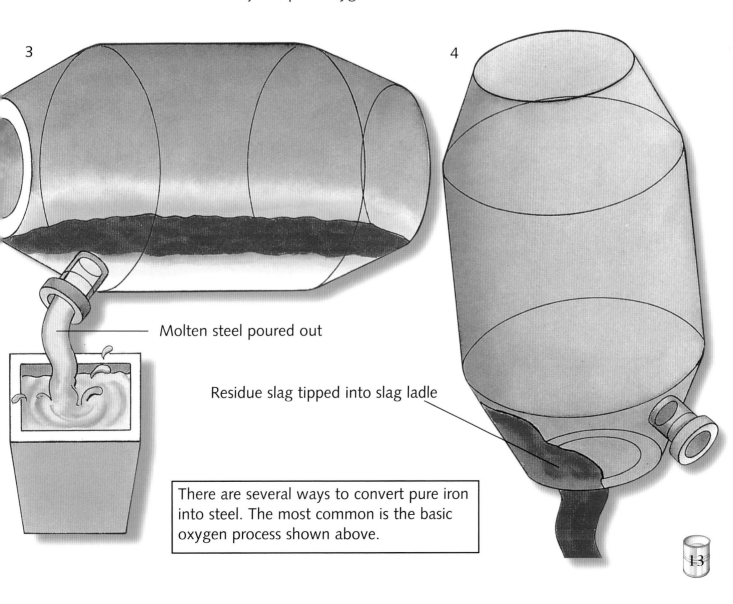

3

4

Molten steel poured out

Residue slag tipped into slag ladle

There are several ways to convert pure iron into steel. The most common is the basic oxygen process shown above.

13

ALUMINIUM

Aluminium is another very important metal. It is light, strong and a good conductor of heat and electricity. Aluminium has historically been used to make cooking pots and electric cables, but the metal is increasingly being used for car manufacturing. Cars made from aluminium parts are lighter and need less fuel to run. Recycled aluminium can also be used to make car components.

'Bauxite' is the principle ore of aluminium. This claylike, earthy substance is found in the Earth's crust. It contains aluminium mixed with a number of chemicals including oxygen. Electricity is used to separate the metal in a process called 'electrolysis'.

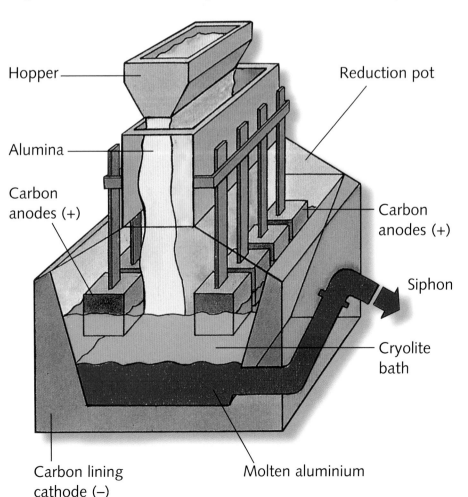

Hopper

Alumina

Carbon anodes (+)

Reduction pot

Carbon anodes (+)

Siphon

Cryolite bath

Carbon lining cathode (–)

Molten aluminium

The electrolysis process
• Molten alumina (aluminium oxide) and cryolite (another aluminium compound) are poured into the reduction pot.
• Alumina is made up of positively charged aluminium particles and negatively charged oxygen particles.
• When electricity is passed through the system, the oxygen moves to the positive carbon 'anodes' while the aluminium collects on the negative 'cathode' floor.
• The pure aluminium can then be siphoned off.

Aluminium can be manufactured into long strips for industrial use

COPPER AND ITS ALLOYS

Copper is one of the oldest known metals. It has great strength and durability. Copper is also:

• a good conductor of heat and electricity, often used to make heating components and electrical cables.

• flexible and resistant to rust, often used to make water pipes and roofs.

• easily recycled and can be used to make a range of very strong alloys.

Copper alloys are being developed all the time for use in technology. For example, car radiators made from copper alloys have been found to be more efficient than those made from aluminium, and can help save on fuel costs.

COPPER

Brass is made from copper and zinc. Brass is an attractive metal and is often used to make decorative items like buttons. Brass is also very hard wearing and ideal for machine parts.
Bronze is copper alloyed with tin. It is highly resistant to corrosion and capable of producing a resonant sound when hit. For this reason bronze is 'cast' to make statues and bells.
Cupronickel is made from copper and nickel. It is shiny, resilient and easy to mould. Many silver-coloured coins are made of this alloy.
Gunmetal is copper alloyed with tin and zinc. It is often used in ship fittings (such as anchor chains) because it is highly resistant to the corrosive effects of salt water.

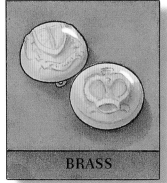

BRASS

BRONZE

CUPRONICKEL

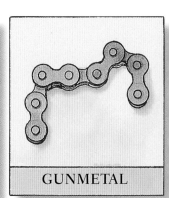

GUNMETAL

Bells are often cast from bronze

MERCURY – LIQUID METAL

Mercury is the only metal which is a liquid at room temperature – it only becomes a solid when the temperature is below -39°C. Nicknamed 'quicksilver' because of the unusual way in which it flows, mercury is also one of the most poisonous elements.

Mercury is particularly sensitive to changes in temperature – expanding when it is heated and contracting as it cools. This makes mercury ideal for use in thermometers and barometers. Metal alloys containing mercury are known as 'amalgams'. Amalgams are often used to make fluorescent lights because they withstand high temperatures and are long-lasting.

This underwater thermometer detects changes in temperature caused by a geothermal vent

Powerful mercury vapour lamps are used to light up sports stadiums

PRECIOUS METALS

Gold, silver and platinum are highly valuable because they are both rare and attractive. These hard-wearing metals are also ideal for making delicate jewellery.

Precious metals have other important practical uses too. Gold is an excellent reflector of light and heat. It is used to coat spacecraft and satellites to protect them from the sun, and to focus light from industrial and medical lasers. Silver is the best conductor of electricity and is used in batteries, fuses and electrical components. Silver is also sensitive to light and used to make photographic film. Platinum withstands extreme temperatures and helps to speed up chemical reactions. Among other things, it is used to make jet engine fuel nozzles and catalytic convertors in cars.

A silversmith making decorative jewellery

Did you know..?

• The chemical symbol for gold is Au. This was taken from the Latin word 'aurum' which means 'shining dawn.'

• Stone age man was the first to fashion gold into jewellery and decorative ornaments.

• Gold and silver are still used as valuable currency. Nowadays coins are made of cheaper alloys, but gold and silver bars (or 'ingots') are still used by banks in special cases.

Gold bars are often stored in vaults. Gold thread (above) can also be used to decorate clothes.

SHAPING METALS

Look at the metal objects around you – perhaps you can see a bicycle wheel, a key or a spoon. Each of these objects has its own special shape. Many metals may appear so hard and strong that it seems impossible to change their form. Powerful machinery, made of even stronger metals, can shape and bend many metals.

When metals are purified they are made into blocks or slabs. The metal can then be shaped to make the many different objects we use. Some metals, such as copper and gold, can be shaped while they are cold. But others, like steel, are more easily shaped when they are red hot.

HOT METAL

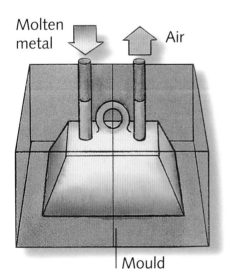

Molten metal · Air · Mould

Casting
Hot liquid metal is poured into a mould where it solidifies. The mould is broken open and the metal 'casting' is released.

Forging
A red hot 'ingot' can be shaped by pounding with a metal 'ram'. Usually the bed of the forge and the ram hold two halves of a mould called a 'die'.

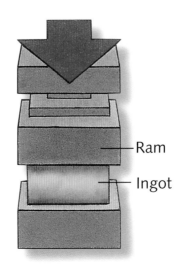

Ram · Ingot

Rolling
A red hot slab may be passed backwards and forwards between rollers. The slab gradually gets longer and thinner – like dough under a rolling pin.

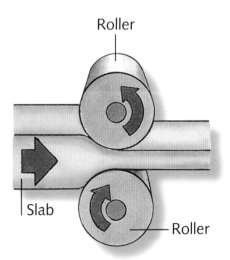

Roller · Slab · Roller

COLD METAL

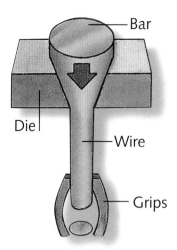

Bar

Die

Wire

Grips

Drawing

A tempered metal rod is pulled through a die. This process is repeated through narrower dies until the rod becomes a long thin wire.

Extrusion

Soft lead alloys can be made into thin-walled tubes by 'extrusion'. When the ram hits the metal, the metal is forced up the sides, forming a tube.

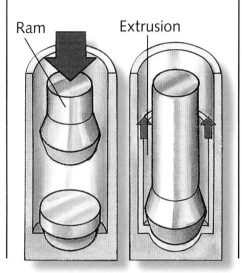

Ram

Extrusion

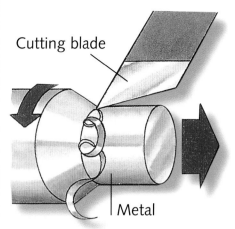

Cutting blade

Metal

Machining

Metal which has been shaped may need to be trimmed in a 'lathe'. The rotating metal is held firmly while a sharp, hard blade trims it.

Cutting lengths of continuously cast steel

CUTTING AND JOINING

Some metal objects can be made from one piece of metal. But others have to be made from a number of different pieces. Metal can be cut with an 'oxyacetylene torch'. This torch uses the gases oxygen and acetylene which burn together at over 3,000° C. This is hot enough to cut through steel by melting it. Lasers are used to concentrate heat and cut through metal very quickly and accurately.

When a metal is heated it can melt. If two almost-melted edges are placed together and allowed to cool, they will form a strong joint called a weld. Riveting and soldering are other permanent ways to join metals.

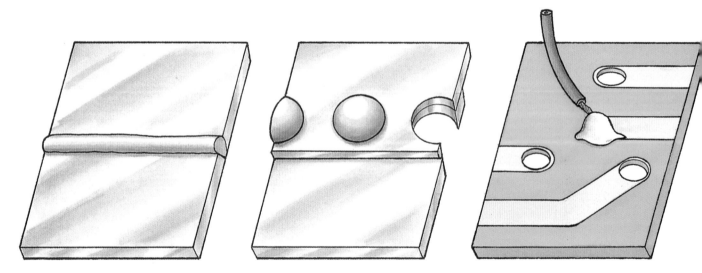

Welding
A gas torch can be used to melt the edges of two pieces of metal. They then fuse together with some added molten metal. When the metals cool they form a strong joint.

Riveting
The rivet is pushed through holes in overlapping plates so that the pointed end pokes through. This end is hammered flat to hold the pieces tightly together.

Soldering
Soldering is used like glue to join delicate pieces of metal. Solder is an alloy of tin, lead and antimony. Molten solder is applied to the joint where it fuses the pieces together.

Cutting through a sheet of metal

THE ENVIRONMENT

Metals are extremely useful for our daily activities. But the process of finding, extracting and refining metals can damage our environment. Furthermore, we live in an age where radioactive metals are widely used. These highly reactive metals combine to give off powerful energy which can be used in industry and for military weapons. The radioactive emissions from these devices can have a devastating effect on our environment.

▼ Wildlife

When metals are extracted from the ground the vegetation and soil covering the deposit are removed. Sometimes a new road is needed to access the site. These actions can cause erosion, destroy wildlife habitats and impair the natural beauty of an area. Aquatic life in nearby water sources may also be affected

▲ Pollution

By their nature, metals are strong and resistant to corrosion. Scrap metal is therefore a serious waste product. It spoils the natural beauty of a landscape. Abandoned cars are a particular problem. Mercury used in car head lamps and antilock breaking systems can release toxic chemicals into the environment, causing harm to human health and wildlife.

◀ Waste metal

Metal is a valuable material and consequently waste metal is rarely deposited in landfill waste sites. Instead this strong and hard-wearing material is reused or recycled again and again. Scrap metal companies have licences that allow them to deposit and store metal in a safe manner. This helps to prevent toxic chemicals from being released into the environment.

▶ Recycling

Recycling metal saves natural resources, uses less energy than the mining process and reduces air and water pollution. Scrap metal recycling is well developed throughout the world. Scrap metal is commonly mixed with 'new' metal to make new products, such as in the steel-making process.

◀ What you can do

Many metal items in your home can be reused or recycled. Recycling aluminium tins and cans is one way that you can help to save energy and conserve the world's natural resources. Old computers and other electrical equipment can also be reused. Why don't you ask about recycling schemes in your local area?

MODERN METALS

Scientists continue to discover and develop new metals and alloys which can be used in modern technology and industry. The aviation industry in particular, requires metals that are strong and light. For this reason aluminium alloys are often used to make planes. Titanium is used for high speed aircraft that get very hot and some engine parts are made of steel. As fossil fuels run out, the search also goes on for lightweight metals that can be used to convert chemical energy into electrical energy. These metals could be used to make batteries or fuel cells.

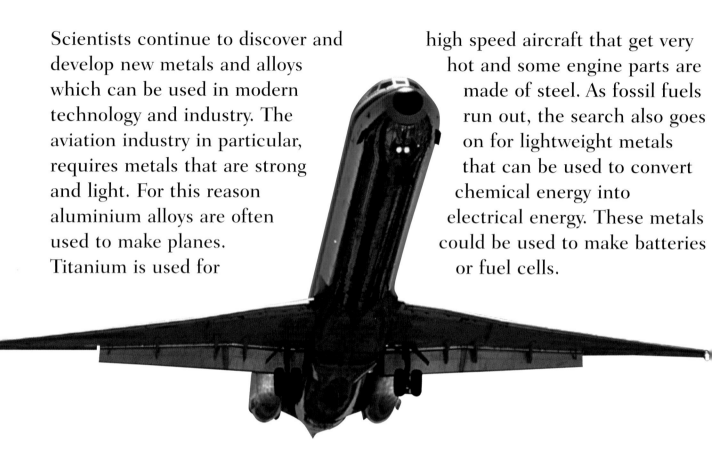

Each metal has its own particular properties. So we may choose different metals to do different jobs. When an electric current passes through tungsten wire it glows but does not melt. This makes it ideal for light bulbs. Forks need to be cheap and strong but must not rust. Stainless steel is a suitable choice. See if you can find out why other metals in these pictures are being used.

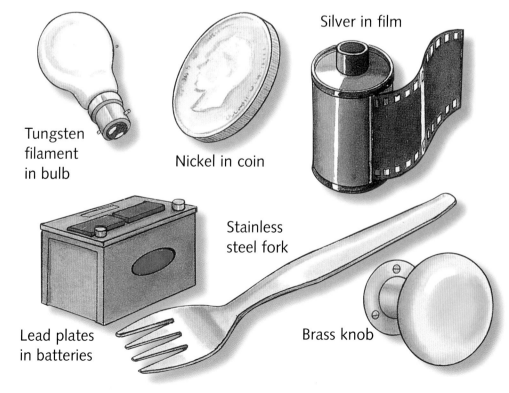

Tungsten filament in bulb

Nickel in coin

Silver in film

Lead plates in batteries

Stainless steel fork

Brass knob

A lot of metals and metal alloys have been used to make this coach. The body and chassis are mostly made of metal. The battery contains lead plates; all the wiring is copper; the trim is probably chromium or stainless steel; and the door handles are plated zinc alloy. The wheels may be an alloy of magnesium and aluminium and the lightbulbs contain tungsten. A catalytic converter, made from rare metals such as palladium, rhodium and platinum, can be placed in the exhaust system to make the engine fumes cleaner. The converter changes polluting gases, such as carbon monoxide, into cleaner substances.

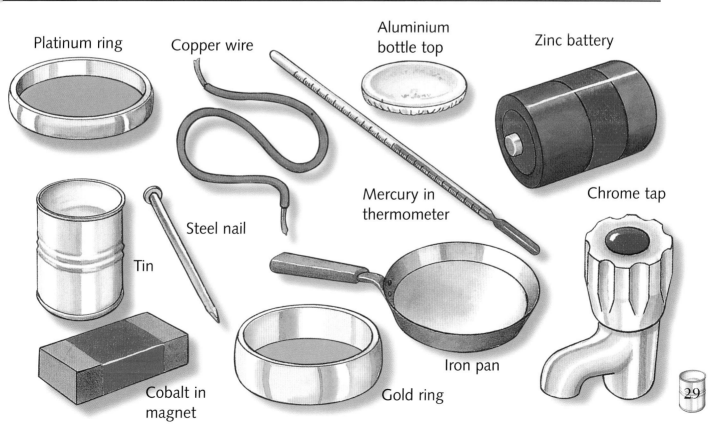

Platinum ring

Copper wire

Aluminium bottle top

Zinc battery

Tin

Steel nail

Mercury in thermometer

Chrome tap

Cobalt in magnet

Iron pan

Gold ring

METAL DEPOSITS

The map below shows where some of the most important metals are mined.

IRON There are vast deposits of iron ore around the world. The largest deposit is at Kursk, about 500 km south of Moscow in the former Soviet Union. It is estimated that this area has over 10 billion tonnes of iron ore reserves. Other large deposits are in the southern Urals, North America and Australia. The two ores which contain the most iron are black 'magnetite' and red 'hematite'.

ALUMINIUM The main aluminium ore is 'bauxite'. It is much more scarce than iron ore and is also more expensive to produce into metal. Cape York, Northern Queensland, Australia has the world's largest bauxite deposits. Here, 25 per cent of the world's aluminium is produced, although Indonesia, Jamaica, Brazil and Western Australia also have huge deposits.

COPPER The 'copperbelt' of Zambia-Democratic Republic of Congo is one of the largest copper ore deposits in the world.

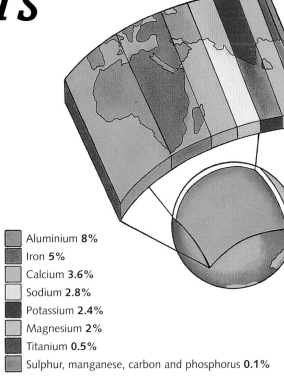

Aluminium **8%**
Iron **5%**
Calcium **3.6%**
Sodium **2.8%**
Potassium **2.4%**
Magnesium **2%**
Titanium **0.5%**
Sulphur, manganese, carbon and phosphorus **0.1%**

Elements in the Earth's crust

Six metals – aluminium, iron, calcium, sodium, potassium and magnesium make up just 24 per cent of the Earth's crust. Oxygen and silicon make up another 75 per cent, leaving only one per cent for all the other naturally-occurring elements in the Earth's crust.

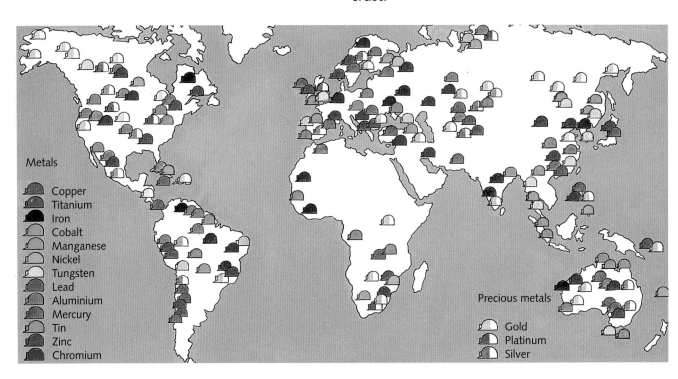

Metals

Copper
Titanium
Iron
Cobalt
Manganese
Nickel
Tungsten
Lead
Aluminium
Mercury
Tin
Zinc
Chromium

Precious metals

Gold
Platinum
Silver

30

GLOSSARY

Alloy
A substance with metallic properties formed by mixing a metal with one or more metals or non metals.

Amalgam
A mixture of mercury and another metal, usually silver.

Anodes
Parts of an electric circuit attached to the positive part of a power supply.

Barometer
An instrument for measuring air pressure.

Blast furnace
An enclosed chamber in which heat is produced to extract a metal from its ore.

Cast
Metals that are shaped in a mould.

Catalyst
A chemical which helps a chemical reaction take place more easily.

Cathode
Part of an electric circuit attached to the negative terminal of a power supply.

Conductor
Something which transfers heat or electricity easily from place to place.

Corrosion
A process in which a solid (particularly metal) is eaten away and changed by a chemical action.

Die
A hard material used to cut or form metal in a press or similar device.

Electrolysis
The passing of electricity through a solution which can cause chemical changes.

Element
A substance that cannot be divided into anything smaller. There are about 100 naturally occurring elements – 70 of which are metals.

Forge
A hearth for melting and shaping metals.

Geologist
One who studies the origin, history, structure and composition of the Earth.

Lasers
Devices which produce intense beams of light.

Magma
Hot melted rock, formed under the Earth's surface.

Magnet
A material that can attract certain substances.

Mineral
A naturally occurring substance with a particular chemical composition.

Mining
The process of extracting from the Earth.

Ore
Any naturally occurring mineral from which metal can be extracted.

Recycling
The process of re-using waste materials to make new products.

Smelting
When a metal is extracted from an ore by heating. This happens in a giant oven called a blast furnace.

INDEX

A
aircraft 28
alloys 12, 16, 29, 31
aluminium 8, 13, 14, 15, 28, 29, 31
amalgams 18, 31
anode 14, 31

B
barometer 18, 31
blast furnace 10, 11, 31
brass 16, 17, 28
bronze 16

C
carbon 10, 13, 14
carbon dioxide 11
carbon monoxide 29
cast 16, 17, 22, 31
catalaytic converter 20, 29
cathode 14, 31
chromium 12, 29
conductor 5, 16, 20, 31
copper 4, 6, 8, 16, 21, 28, 29
corrosion 26, 31
cupronickel 16

D
drawing 23
dredging 8, 9
duralumin 28
dynamite 8

E
Earth 4, 6, 8, 30
electricity 14, 16
electrolysis 14, 16, 31
environment 26, 27
explosives 8
extrusion 23

F
forging 22, 31

G
geologist 6, 31
gold 6, 8, 20, 21, 30
gunmetal 16

I
ingots 21
iron 6, 8, 10, 11, 12, 13, 30

J
jewellery 20

L
lasers 24, 31
lava 7
lead 28, 29, 30
lime 13
limestone 7, 11

M
magma 6, 31
magnesium 29
Malaysia 9
melt 10
mercury 18, 19, 29, 30
minerals 6, 7, 31
miners 8
mining 6, 8, 31
molten 7, 11, 14, 24

N
nickel 28, 30

O
open-cast mining 8, 9
ores 6, 8, 11, 31
oxygen 10, 11, 13, 14, 24

P
platinum 20, 30
poisonous 18
pollution 26
precious 20

Q
quicksilver 18

R
recycling 27, 31
riveting 24
rocks 4, 6, 7, 8
rolling 22

S
silver 20, 28, 30
silversmith 20
slag 11, 13
smelting 10, 14, 31
soldering 24
South Africa 8
stainless steel 12, 28, 29
steel 10, 12, 13, 22 ,23, 24, 28, 29

T
thermometers 18
tin 9, 16, 29, 30
tungsten 28, 29, 30

U
underground mining 8

W
welding 24
wildlife 26

Z
zinc 16, 29, 30